HOW TO GO FROM THE 99% INTO THE 1%

HOW TO LIVE YOUR AMERICAN DREAM

KURT D. CAMBIER

Publisher's Disclaimer

While the publisher and coauthors have used their best efforts in preparing this book, they make no representations or warranties with respect to the accuracy or completeness of the contents of this book. Nothing in this book should be construed as offering legal, tax, or financial advice. No warranty may be created or extended by sales representatives or written sales materials. The advice and strategies contained herein may not be suitable for your situation. You should consult with a professional where appropriate. Neither the publisher nor the authors shall be liable for any loss of profit or any other commercial damages, including but not limited to special, incidental, consequential or other damages.

Created and produced in Atlanta, Georgia, USA
First Edition, Volume 1

TABLE OF CONTENTS

INTRODUCTION..1

CHAPTER 1: I WASN'T BORN ON THIRD BASE
THINKING I HIT A TRIPLE 3

CHAPTER 2: THE 4 P'S 13

CHAPTER 3: PURPOSE..15

CHAPTER 4: PATIENCE...21

CHAPTER 5: PASSION 23

CHAPTER 6: PARTICULAR KNOWLEDGE.................27

CHAPTER 7: PAYING YOURSELF FIRST 32

CHAPTER 8: HOW NUMBERS CAN BE MISLEADING
....35

CHAPTER 9: OUR PROCESS...41

CHAPTER 10: PLANNING CIRCLE 45

CHAPTER 11: NEXT STEPS...50

INTRODUCTION

This book is being written to help those who dream, those who strive for excellence, those who wish to leave the world a better place when their time is up. It is written for those that want to leave their mark on the world. This book is written for the entrepreneur in all of us. Whether you are creating a vision or leading your family, all of us are entrepreneurs of some kind.

Many of us dream, but a dream is just a wish without a plan and without action! Remember, cowards never start, and the weak have died along the way. Frontrunners run the hardest and risk the most. If they see an open shot, they take it. Always remember, you miss all the shots you do not take.

Innovators and creative visionaries are not afraid of failure. Our defeats make us stronger, and our failures make us wiser. Never be afraid to fail.

Complacent happiness is dangerous – it dulls the senses.

The act of competing is the act of forgetting your limits, your doubts, your pain and your past. The good Lord put eyes in the front of our heads so we can see where we are going, not where we have been.

As humans, we are either growing or we are dying. My hope is by reading this book I help you grow.

CHAPTER 1

I WASN'T BORN ON THIRD BASE THINKING I HIT A TRIPLE

One of the reasons why I'm so intent on keeping history alive – in keeping the stories of my family close to my heart – is that my own history has heavily influenced my trajectory. Without my history, and without my struggles, my success never would have come to pass. And it's not just my history that I work to honor. My family history plays a large part in how I strive to live my life and to bring success to my clients.

When my mother, Virginia Cambier, was only two years old, her mother died of breast cancer. Her father was an illiterate German immigrant who was, in a short time, widowed and left to care for his seven children. He quickly became overwhelmed with the considerable responsibilities left to him. Because he was uneducated, unprepared, and burdened with a lack of understanding of the English language, he had his farm in Minnesota quit claim deeded away from him by a neighbor. He knew he could no longer sustain the health and welfare of his children, so he drove my mother and her siblings down from Minnesota to my great grandfather's farm in Remsen, Iowa.

Already in his late 60s, my great grandfather wasn't necessarily in a better place to care for his late daughter's children. He did what he could, putting all seven in a Catholic orphanage in Sioux City, Iowa, and paid a monthly fee in exchange for the assurance that none of his grandchildren would be adopted out, and that way the family would stay together. I remember visiting that orphanage as a child in the late '60s, and I remember how my mother chuckled when she heard they were closing the orphanage because it was too crowded.

At the time it closed, it only housed 65 children. In my mother's day, the Depression era, the orphanage housed around 360 children. My mother told me how the mattresses were scattered all over the gymnasium floor, and everyone slept side by side, with the boys on one side of the gym and the girls on the other. It was standard practice, at that time, to release the boys at age 12 and the girls at age 15, when the hormones began to rage, so that the orphanage wouldn't have any more children to take care of. My mother was able to arrange that she be released at age 12, along with her twin brother Virgil. They lived in Remsen, Iowa, with their aunt, Clara Gossling, who was a true saint. She never married, and yet cared for all of those children. When my mother was 18, she attended Briar Cliff College in

Sioux City, Iowa, to begin her education to become a schoolteacher. Soon after, tragedy struck her again. She contracted polio and was told by her doctor that she would never walk again. True to her fighting spirit, she overcame her disease to prove the doctors wrong.

After marrying my father, she had two miscarriages, the last coming after an appendicitis attack when my sister Debbie, who only lived three days, was born prematurely. My mother continued fighting to make a family, ultimately giving birth to four children. My sister Carla was born five years after my mother began her battle with breast cancer. I was ten years old when she passed away. Watching my mother fight and suffer for five years, trying to be with her children, left a profound mark on my life.

My father was a rebel who dropped out of school in the 9th grade and moved away to live on his own at the age of 14. He began working for the railroad, then in a packing plant, before becoming a long-haul truck driver, which he did for 15 years. An eternal entrepreneurial spirit, he put all of his chips on the table and started Cambier Ready Mix in Alton, Iowa. The ready mix business led to the formation of Midwest Precast, a leading agricultural construction company. In it's best year, 1979, he employed 100 people and grossed $7 million in revenue. He thought it was never going to end, but it did. When the farm crisis of the 1980s hit, it destroyed my father's business of 14 years. Suddenly he found himself without money, uneducated, and defeated. On December 30, 1984, he suffered a massive heart attack. I remember the day well, because it was my birthday, and I had just moved to Colorado. I answered the phone that night, and they were calling the family in because he wasn't expected to make it. I spent the night tossing and turning, alone in a strange place. That was a long and lonely night.

But just like my mother, my father was a fighter. The doctors told him he needed a heart transplant and would only live six months. He never got the transplant, took 24 pills and three shots of insulin daily, had only 25% of his heart working, and lived another five years. My father died the same week I met Jeannette, the woman who would become my wife. God truly does work in mysterious, but meaningful ways. When I lost one person I loved, he brought a new one into my life.

This leads me to the story of how I got to Colorado, became a

CFP, ChFC, ® and a partner with Centennial Capital Partners. I had my own life-and-death struggle at the age of 12. In the summer between 7th and 8th grade, I suffered a ruptured appendix. The organ leaked poison, which spread throughout my body, leaving me gravely ill. The surgeons told my father that they didn't know if I would make it out of surgery. I spent the next three months of that summer in and out of the hospital, and I went from a strapping 120 pounds down to a frail 80 pounds. When all the other boys were growing and maturing, my body was fighting to survive. I entered high school a 5'1", 110-pound weakling (quite a contrast to my 6'3" frame today!), and I was known as "Kurt the Squirt."

But ultimately the groundwork had been laid for my fighting spirit. I left Iowa after my father's business failed and my own attempt at an enterprise failed. After I graduated from the University of South Dakota, I borrowed money and invested in a take-and-bake pizza franchise in Spencer, Iowa, known as Pizza Unlimited. I had the fifth-best performing store out of 68 in the franchise chain. Unfortunately, the farm crisis had hit, farms were foreclosed on (more banks failed in the 1980s than in 2008), and I went broke. I loaded everything I had in my car and drove to Colorado, where I worked a few odd construction jobs before landing in Denver with $14 in my pocket, no job, and no place to live. The year was 1984, and I was driving a 1964 Plymouth Valiant. I found a place to live, began working as one of those dreaded telemarketers selling Time Life Books. It was part-time work that allowed me to earn enough to live on, and yet afforded me the time to find a full-time job. Eventually I got hired by an insurance company to sell insurance. I knew no one, so I would grab a handful of business cards and go out on Saturday mornings and knock on doors. Eventually one thing led to another. I became a member of the Million Dollar Round Table, then Court of the Table of the Million Dollar Round Table and many Presidents and Leaders clubs along the way.

Along the way, Jeannette became my wife and gave birth to our three beautiful children: Kameron,

Christian and our daughter Carsen. Shortly after Carsen was born, Jeannette became sick. After weeks of tests, doctors narrowed her illness down to three things: cancer, lupus or multiple sclerosis, eventually narrowing it down further to MS, the effects of which we live with today. It was a scary time period, to have three young children and not know the fate of my wife. It gave me a clearer understanding of how my father must have felt when my mother was ill.

With all the things that have happened to me, I still feel as though I'm a very blessed man. I have a loving family, great business partners, and a group of clients that I truly love and care for. It pains me greatly when I hear of people in my profession who have misled clients or roped them into elaborate Ponzi-schemes, stealing their life savings. I take to heart the words of my father when he spoke of providing a service: "Do what you say you're going to do when you say you're going to do it."

He was a very wise man. He also once told me, "Son, if you remember that the world owes you nothing, then you will be fine." I have hit a few triples in my day, but I certainly wasn't born on third base.

CHAPTER 2

THE 4 P'S

After 3 decades of working in the financial services industry, I have had the great opportunity to meet and learn from some amazing people.

In the coming chapters I will share with you much of the wisdom and knowledge I learned from these great people, many of whom are not worth just millions, or even tens of millions, but in some cases hundreds of millions. What has stood out the most to me is they are not the smartest people I have met nor even the most worldly. What they do possess is an incredible vision, along with a laser focus, an unbreakable passion for what they believe to be right, and they are experts in their fields. It may not be your goal to be wealthy. Maybe your goal is to have an impact through mission work or to leave this place better than you found it, or to give the ones you love the life they deserve. The process is all the same.

To begin the process of moving from the 99% into the 1%, you will need to understand the 4 P's of success.

The 4 P's are:

Purpose

Patience

Passion

Particular knowledge

We will approach this the same way we approach financial planning with our clients. It's a four-step process. So let's move on to the first of the P's: Purpose.

CHAPTER 3

PURPOSE

First, let's take a look at what is a "purpose" and what isn't a "purpose".

What a purpose isn't is anything that is selfishly directed toward yourself. Something like "My purpose is to become rich". That is a recipe for failure.

A true purpose is something like, "Why am I here?" "What is my contribution to mankind?" "How can I make the world a better place?" "How can I take better care of my family and the people I love?"

In order to truly move into the 1%, you have to live larger than yourself. Once you discover what your purpose is, that's the beginning.

Think big here. This is the launching pad. God only created one of you. You are a loving, caring, creative gift to mankind. Share your light, share your gift, and share your love.

Your purpose could be many things. Maybe you want to cure an illness that ravages the world. I have a friend who wants to cure cancer in his lifetime. He is a genius, has aligned himself with Nobel Prize-winning scientists, has his own research lab, and is highly competitive and owns several world records in athletic competitions. He is taking his genius and his competitive spirit with him every day working towards his goal. I would not bet against him. I am friends with someone who saw why her own family plumbing business was failing. She fixed the problem, wrote out a detailed business plan, and franchised the process across America. Not only did she become enormously successful, but she helped others prosper along the way.

Look around you. Someone had to come up with the idea of Netflix, Amazon, Facebook, and Uber. Someone has to change the world. Why not you?

Once you discover your purpose, it's time to develop and implement your plan. Remember, a purpose without a plan is just a dream.

What should you consider when making a plan? The "what." What is your purpose? What is it that is better? What causes it to solve a larger problem? What is the problem it solves? What kind of capital will be required? What time frame? What will be the obstacles?

The "where." Where is this going to happen? Where can you start? Where is the best market for what you want to provide?

Then we move into the areas of systems and processes. The most successful people and businesses I know have processes or systems that are repeatable. They are so refined and defined that they can be repeated by not just them, but anyone who is motivated to do so.

If you can systemize every process of your business from A to Z, have a written plan on how it can be done, you increase the profitability of your business and ultimately maximize the value upon selling the enterprise.

Systems are everything from hiring/firing employees, answering phones, greeting customers, the sales process, the manufacturing process, customer service, social media, farming prospects, marketing, branding, record keeping, accounting – everything must be included in a well-written and structured business plan.

Being repeatable here is the key, repeatable by someone other than the founder.

Here are examples of a couple of friends whom I attended college with back at the University of South Dakota:

In 1984, two college buddies of mine started a small retail mattress firm. On the surface, selling mattresses doesn't sound very exciting. However, these two guys understood the marketplace, developed a repeatable system of marketing, advertising, inventory control, locations, concentration of stores, delivery times, accounting – everything. They knew their numbers, developed a repeatable process, and turned that little retail mattress store into the national giant The Mattress Firm. Obviously, it was a great success, and they became very wealthy.

Another example is of a friend who became very wealthy buying real estate, mainly apartments and commercial property. Another one started buying farmland. In both cases, these guys didn't accumulate millions, or even tens of millions, but these guys grew to hundreds of millions. How? First of all, they understood their numbers - revenues, expenses, and profits. They kept a cushion of cash and credit lines to weather the inevitable economic storms. In both cases they describe their process as simple, boring, cookie cutter; in other words, repeatable.

CHAPTER 4

PATIENCE

To be a patient person is truly a gift. This is probably my biggest character flaw. Patience will allow you to stay on plan, not become irrational. Remember, moving from the 99% to the 1% is hard work. Not all of us are born in the pole position in life. Some of us start further back in the pack, but the good news is, the race of life is a long one for most of us.

Remember, Ray Kroc started McDonalds at the age of 53. Warren Buffet made two-thirds of his wealth after the age of 55.

I believe hard work is a blessing from God. The things that challenge us the most are the things that separate us from others. It's our challenges and our defeats that lead us to our greatness.

You can't skip steps on your way to moving into the 1%. If you do, you will always be mired in the masses of the 99%.

You have to look at your purpose like you look at your children. You have to allow your children the time to mature, grow up, make mistakes, and yet ultimately surprise you with their success. Your purpose is your child. You must mold it and let it grow and mature and take on a life of its own.

Only through patience can you stick to your plan and see your purpose change the world.

CHAPTER 5

PASSION

Passion is the fire that burns within. Remember, fire creates its own wind. It's that wind that will inspire you to learn more and work longer and harder than others. Remember, without the fire there is no wind, and without the wind, there may be no fire.

Find ways to keep the fire lit. For me, it's a daily practice of rising early. I usually wake up at 4:00 a.m. I exercise and listen to music that inspires me. Most mornings I go for an eight-mile hike. It is my spiritual time. It's the process of putting my game face on for the day. Passion is the fuel that powers the engine of your life.

When I coached youth sports, I told the young kids I coached to remember three things: 1. Always smile. 2. The thoughts you have in your head today will determine the person you become tomorrow. 3. Always give more than what you get.

Let's look at these individually. Smile. Something happens to people when they smile. Positive endorphins permeate throughout their body. No one wants to be around a sourpuss, a whiner. If you want to attract people who are positive, then SMILE.

The thoughts you have in your head today will determine the person you will become tomorrow. Study someone you truly admire and respect. Mimic their actions. Imitation is the ultimate form of flattery. Research the people you admire the most, those which, perhaps, have used their purpose to change the world. See yourself as the success you want to be. How does that make you feel? This instills confidence, and confidence is your power to overcome doubt.

Always be willing to give more than what you get. Be spontaneously generous. It will become natural. Be a giving, loving, selfless person that others will naturally be attracted to.

If we lived in a world of selfless giving, how great would the world be? If you are willing to love the people around you, you will have more love, more friendships. You will find more kindness, more success, and ultimately more happiness. Karma is real. You give out love, you get love back. You give out hatred, anger, frustration, and that will come back to you. I run my marriage this way: I wake up each day asking myself, "What can I do to make her day better?" Truthfully, 90% of the time the answer is get away from her and go to work. It is the little things that mean the most: Listening when it really matters, an unexpected note or text or message, an act of kindness or love. My marriage has been easy because I have always been willing to give more than I get.

My life has been full of laughter and joy. My motto is to Live Large, Laugh Often, Love Always and Pay It Forward when you can. Because of this attitude I have appeared on National TV, Fox Business, CNBC, shared the stage with Legends like Astronaut Buzz Aldrin, Lt. General Russell Honore, been on stage at the Harvard Faculty Club, and met leaders who are changing the world.

CHAPTER 6

PARTICULAR KNOWLEDGE

The distinguishing characteristic that I have noticed high achievers all possess is a high degree of knowledge in the field of their passion. All knowledge can be broken into two types: Horizontal and Vertical.

Horizontal knowledge refers to someone who knows a little about a lot. This type of individual tends to be more extroverted, very well educated, and modestly successful; someone who is willing to share their wealth of knowledge in any area without any real expertise. We refer to Horizontal knowledge as knowing a little about a lot.

Vertical knowledge refers to someone who has deep knowledge in the area of their expertise or passion. They know a lot about a little. They have become the authority in the area their career path has taken them. Often they seem introverted, even quiet, unconfident, often mistaken for perhaps unintelligent and not very worldly. However, when the subject of their passion comes up, they become extroverted, perhaps obnoxiously so, and delve deep into the topic that drives their passion. Remember, if you become the best at what you do, people will line up and pay you a great deal of money to tap into your expertise. This is hard work but very well worth the effort.

It can take years to develop the Vertical knowledge needed to be seen as the leading authority in a particular field. Experience is not enough. Many people say they have 30 years of experience, but in reality what they really have is a year of experience repeated 30 times; in other words, they've never expanded their knowledge. Vertical knowledge is created after many hours of work and many hours of burning the midnight oil. It is spending weekends dedicating yourself to improving your craft or trade. This is where visions and dreams are born, become infants, grow into children, and then ultimately into mature adults.

Once you have particular knowledge, Vertical knowledge, then you have to brand yourself or your company to promote that knowledge. Self-promotion will be required at this point until your reputation is more widely known. Branding by name, process, system – something that can be easily recognized by those who would benefit from your wisdom and expertise.

It has often been said there are no natural born geniuses, but that genius is self-made, self-taught. It has been widely believed it takes 10,000 hours to master your craft. Simply put, there is no substitute for hard work and self sacrifice.

Branding. Yes, what you call yourself makes a difference. People who have an entrepreneurial spirit also tend to possess a large ego. How do I know this? I am one of them. People in my profession, the profession of finance, have tended to name their businesses after themselves. I was guilty of this. Early on I was known as the Cambier Investment Group, LTD. Not a very descriptive, transferable, repeatable brand. We are now known as Centennial Capital Partners "Wealth Management Strategies for Select Individuals", a name easier to expand and transfer. You want your name to give some indication of what you do. If possible, it should represent your process or unique value proposition. The most powerful branding helps you be seen as the authority or expert in your field.

Whether it be living the life of an entrepreneur, working in your chosen field or mission, or being the head of your family, the fundamentals of the 4 P's are all the same. To be successful, you must have a purpose, you must be patient, live with passion, and always keep learning more about your particular field of knowledge. Once you lay the groundwork for your future success, you must learn to pay yourself first.

CHAPTER 7

PAYING YOURSELF FIRST

Once you lay the groundwork for your future success, you must learn to pay yourself first.

As we go through life, we often struggle to find the time to do much more than just make it through the day. Driving in traffic, handling the day's tasks at work, getting to our kids' or grandkids' programs or games, there is just not time left for much else.

One of the things we have to do is to pay ourselves first. I do not mean this just in financial terms but in terms of life itself. In my own personal life I have come to the realization that as I've grown older and life became more complicated and there were larger demands for my time, I had to learn to pay myself first.

I found my health to be my number one concern. I also found that if I waited until after work to exercise, I was too exhausted to do it. So what I learned to do was pay myself first by getting up early to exercise. I usually hike 8 miles in two hours before I start my workday. I have found this to be both physically and mentally stimulating. Physically I feel alive, and mentally my stress melts away.

I also have found this to be true with my financial life. I have learned to pay myself first and pay everyone else after that. What that means is save money, invest for your future, and adjust your lifestyle. Here is a brief story to illustrate this point:

Say you're at a Saturday afternoon matinee with your family. The theatre is packed. You notice quite a few familiar faces. The gentleman who sold you your new car is there with his family. The lady from the furniture store where you just purchased a new sofa is there with her family. As you settle in to watch the movie, you begin to smell smoke. All of a sudden someone yells "Fire!" You stand up, tell your family to stay put, and go help get everyone else out of the burning theatre, and then you come back and help your family out last. Of course we wouldn't do that, but by paying everyone else first and trying to save what is left, we are, in essence, doing just that. To be successful and live a great, well-planned life, we must adjust our lifestyle such that we can pay ourselves first and others last.

CHAPTER 8

HOW NUMBERS CAN BE MISLEADING

How we look at numbers can have a dramatic effect on our investment success. First we need to understand the difference between real and stated returns. We will use the chart below to demonstrate our point (Chart 1).

	Low Standard Deviation Portfolio	High Average Return Portfolio
STARTING VALUE	$1,000,000	$1,000,000
Year 1	5%	7%
Year 2	7%	19%
Year 3	8%	15%
Year 4	-6%	-38%
Year 5	8%	22%
Year 6	7%	18%
Year 7	11%	38%
Year 8	9%	14%
Year 9	-8%	-45%
Year 10	7%	27%
Ending Value	$1,569,832	$1,436,192
Average Return	5%	8%
Standard Deviation	6%	27%

* This chart is for illustrative purposes only and is not representative of any specific investment or mix of investments.

We have two portfolios: One is low deviation (volatility) and one is high deviation (volatility). Of course, the low volatility portfolio has less gains on the upside but less losses on the downside. The high deviation portfolio has a 60% higher return than the low deviation portfolio; 8% compared to 5%, but because the high deviation portfolio experienced massive losses, it ended up with less money. This is because it takes huge gains to recoup huge losses. We are taught in school that -50 and +50 equals 0, but in reality, if you have $1,000,000 and lose $500,000 (50%), you have $500,000. If you gain back 50%, you are only at $750,000. In fact, you would have to earn 100% on that 50% loss just to get back to even. See Chart 2 below to understand the dramatic loss/gain numbers.

AMOUNT OF LOSS	RETURN REQUIRED TO BREAKEVEN	# OF YEARS TO BREAKEVEN WITH ANNUAL RETURN OF 10%*
-10%	11.1%	1.1
-15%	17.7%	1.7
-20%	25.0%	2.3
-25%	33.3%	3.0
-30%	42.9%	3.7
-35%	53.9%	4.5
-40%	66.7%	5.4
-45%	81.8%	6.3
-50%	100.0%	7.3

*10% was chosen as a reference to the long-term annualized return of the S&P 500 Index. The chart above is hypothetical for illustrative purposes only.

The bigger the loss, the bigger the return needed, and it will take longer just to get even.

Chart 3 below represents the importance of the sequence of returns:

Age	Annual Return	Portfolio A Year End Balance	Annual Return	Portfolio B Year End Balance
66	32%	$635,000	-37%	$290,000
67	-3%	$590,200	5%	$278,750
68	30%	$740,738	16%	$296,828
69	8%	$772,678	5%	$284,351
70	10%	$821,808	11%	$287,492
71	1%	$801,045	29%	$341,882
72	38%	$1,075,590	-22%	$236,817
73	23%	$1,292,229	-12%	$177,652
74	33%	$1,686,996	-9%	$129,994
75	29%	$2,143,605	21%	$124,673
76	21%	$2,560,164	29%	$127,231
77	-9%	$2,295,144	33%	$134,611
78	-12%	$1,984,082	23%	$129,928
79	-22%	$1,510,871	38%	$142,587
80	29%	$1,911,209	1%	$106,198
81	11%	$2,082,492	10%	$77,869
82	5%	$2,146,499	8%	$43,981
83	16%	$2,448,618	30%	$15,854
84	5%	$2,528,488	-3%	$0
85	-37%	$1,549,110	32%	$0
Average Return	**10.4%**		**10.4%**	

* The performance shown is based on the assumptions listed above and is for Illustrative purposes only and is not based on any actual client account. The yearly income distribution starts at $25,000 and is compounded yearly with 3% inflation.

In this chart we have two portfolios. Both portfolios start with $500,000 and both earn a 20-year average return of 10.4% Both have a withdraw of $25,000 adjusted for an annual inflation increase of 3%. The only difference is the order of the returns is switched. Portfolio A experiences early positive returns and then losses in later years. Portfolio B experiences early losses and then positive returns in later years. Portfolio A has $1,549,110 in it. Portfolio B has $0. Why is that? It is the importance of the sequence of returns.

Let's use this example: I come from Iowa and grew up in the heart of America's agriculture country. A farmer has fixed expenses he must cover each year, much like a retiree has fixed expenses they must cover. A farmer is subjected to many things out of his control; weather, commodity prices, etc., much like the retiree is subject to economic forces or market forces that they have no control over.

If a farmer has a bad year because of poor weather or low crop prices, he has to sell something to cover his expenses. If he sells farmland, he has less land to plant next year and every year after that, leading to a lifetime of lower income. This is much like the retiree selling principal in down years to cover expenses. They may never recover, resulting in a lifetime of lower income. In investing this is known as a negative drawdown. It can be life altering.

CHAPTER 9

OUR PROCESS

Over the three decades I have been in the financial services industry I have learned many things and some the hard way.

Let's talk about the process of three different buckets with three different looks, three different designs and three different goals (Chart 4).

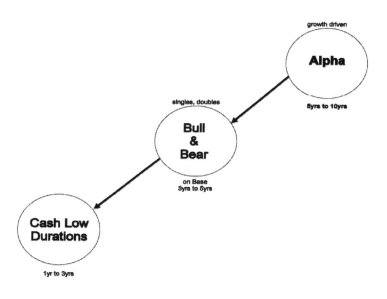

The main bucket, our core bucket, is the design of a bull and bear portfolio. An easy way to remember this is a bull attacks upward and a bear attacks downward.

Our portfolios are back-tested for risk as well as for upside capture and downside capture. We use cutting-edge technology in assembling these investment designs. The goal of the core portfolio is to take moderate levels of risk and get lower volatility returns. We refer to this as hitting singles and doubles and maybe an occasional triple. The best teams in baseball are the ones that have the highest on-base percentages. We want our clients on base so that when the opportunity comes, we can score runs. We refer to this as our 3-to-5-year time horizon portfolios.

On the longer-term portfolios we have what we call our Alpha bucket. Alpha in investment vernacular is referring to processes that may bring superior long-term returns. The opportunity for long-term performance often comes with higher volatility. This portfolio is considered a 5-to-10-year portfolio. With time, short-term market volatility gets mitigated the longer the investment horizon.

The example I will use here is a slinky (spring). If you hold a slinky (spring) in your hands close together and swing it, the movement is quite significant. If you hold your arms further apart and stretch the slinky (spring), the movement is much less. We are trying to grow our Alpha portfolio to feed our core portfolio.

For our third bucket we implement our short-term, low volatility, conservative income bucket. This bucket is designed to pay out 1 to 3 years of income needs to lessen the threat of a negative drawdown. It, of course, is fed by our core bucket. So, in summary, our more aggressive bucket is a 5-to-10-year time horizon that ultimately feeds our low volatility bucket that provides our desired income. These are designed and backtested to help us maximize our opportunities for success. How much we put in each bucket is customized to your needs, risk tolerance, and time horizons.

CHAPTER 10

PLANNING CIRCLE

As a Certified Financial Planner, my role is to help my clients make wise decisions that lead to success. The process is called the Planning Circle. What is the Planning Circle? It all starts with the planning horizon. The planning horizon is much like standing on a beach looking out over the ocean. Above the ocean are things you see, but you know that below the surface are things you do not see. Whether you are putting together a plan for your next entrepreneurial idea or your own personal financial plan, the process is the same.

The above-the-horizon issues are your visions, your dreams, your mission. This is true whether you are working on a business plan or a personal financial plan. It is the why of what you want to do or accomplish. Below the horizon is the mechanics, the systems, the processes implemented to get you to your above-the-horizon dreams. In business planning it is the systems, the processes, the branding, and the repeatability of the entire business operation. In personal financial planning it is the process of knowing when you want to retire, how much is needed, how it should be invested, how long it will need to last . . . everything.

Mission, Vision, Values, Goals

What? Why? Who? How?

The Planning Strategies, Tactics and Tools of the
Planning Circle

The Planning Circle is broken down into 4 steps:

1. Identifying and clarifying the problem

2. Creative solutions leading to decisions

3. Implementation of the solution leading to
    results

4. Managing the results leading to confidence

Step 1: Clarifying the Problem

Here is where the problem or concern is
diagnosed. If you are innovating a new business
solution, what problem will it solve? If you are
doing a personal financial plan, where are your
shortcomings? In either case, you have to

thoroughly study an issue to understand how to fix it and make it better.

Step 2: Creative Solutions Leading to Decisions

What idea, what process can you use to solve the problem? What behavior must you change to reach your financial goals? What are the yearly, monthly, weekly, daily goals you must meet to achieve the desired outcome you wish to have? Do you know your numbers? Do you know your budget? Is the solution repeatable to others? Is the family all in?

Step 3: Implementation of the Solution Leading to Results

This is the action plan, putting things into motion, establishing the plan, implementing the investments leading to success.

Step 4: Managing the Results Leading to Confidence:

Reviewing, adjusting, adopting changes as time goes by. This is a living and breathing document. Know your numbers, follow the money, understand your profit margins. What is working? What isn't? Who are the rainmakers in your organization and who is dead weight? Look for accountability here, both in your organization and in yourself. Complacency that follows success is always the thing that destroys a seemingly strong organization. Remember, you either grow or you die; there is nothing in between.

In your personal financial planning, this is where you review the plan, update any changes, and see if you are on point or whether you need to change your investments, invest more money, or perhaps spend less and save more.

CHAPTER 11

NEXT STEPS

If you read this book, then either a friend gave it to you or you got it from me. Either way I hope that it has a positive impact on you as a person, whether you ever talk to me or not.

My hope is that you give me a call and see how I can help you achieve your American dream. There's no cost or obligation in the initial conversations.

My philosophy is to "Live Large, Laugh Often, Love Always, and Pay it Forward when you can."

Living Large is participating in the world around you, enjoying life, helping others enjoy their lives. Laugh Often. Too many people take themselves too seriously. Learn to laugh more, let your frustrations bounce off of you. Love Always is the most important thing. If you give out love, you get love back; if you give out anger and frustration, guess what you get back? Anger and frustration.

My three principles of living a fulfilling life are, first off, I believe we should go through life with a smile on our faces. No one wants to be around a complaining sourpuss. Be a beacon of light to those around you. Secondly, the thoughts you have in your head today will lead you to the person you will become tomorrow. See yourself as that person, visualize how it will feel being the success you dream about being. Act as if you have already arrived. Find that person you want to be and emulate them. Thirdly, always be willing to give more than you get. If you do this, you will have more friends, more success, more money than you could ever imagine having. The Law of Attraction is alive and well in our universe. Karma is real. Practice this and see what happens in your life.

When you come into my office, these are some of the financial coaching services I help people with:

- Review your designated beneficiaries on life insurance, retirement accounts, and other accounts

- Review the risk on your investment portfolios

- Review the tax efficiency of your investments and how it will affect you in retirement

- Review your retirement income distribution plans

- Review the hidden costs and charges on your current investments

- Review your estate planning documents and coordinate with the appropriate attorneys

There are several other financial related services that I offer all of my clients, so please call my office to set an appointment.

Also, I have a philosophy to always try to give more than what I get in return. If you want to get together and discuss anything in this book or what's going on in your life, then contact me at:

Kurt D. Cambier, CFP, ChFC ®

Centennial Capital Partners

13984 W. Bowles Ave., Suite 102 I Littleton, CO 80127

Phone 303.271.1067 I Fax 303.951.5990I Cell 303.668.3187

Registered Representative, Securities offered through Cambridge Investment Research, Inc., a Broker/Dealer, Member FINRA & SIPC. Investment Advisor Representative, Cambridge Investment Research Advisors, Inc., a Registered Investment Advisor, Cambridge Investment Research and Centennial Capital Partners are not affiliated.

Made in the USA
Columbia, SC
28 October 2020

23660945R00033